Beside
That
Windmill

Beside That Windmill

Illustrated by Don L. Parks
Story by Minda Parks

TEXAS TECH UNIVERSITY PRESS

This book is typeset in Petrona. The paper used in this book meets the minimum requirements of ANSI/NISO Z39.48-1992 (R1997).♾

Designed by Hannah Gaskamp

Library of Congress Cataloging-in-Publication Data

Names: Parks, Minda, 1944– author. | Parks, Don L., 1943– illustrator. Title: Beside That Windmill / Don L. Parks, Minda Parks. Description: Lubbock, Texas: Texas Tech University Press, [2022] | Audience: Ages 4–8 | Audience: Grades K–1 | Summary: "A picture book, featuring windmills particularly, of a young boy's life on a Texas ranch"— Provided by publisher.
Identifiers: LCCN 2022002402 | ISBN 978-1-68283-144-1 (cloth)
Subjects: LCSH: Parks, Don L., 1943—Juvenile literature. | Ranchers—Texas—Biography—Juvenile literature. | CYAC: Windmills | Ranch life Classification: LCC TJ823 .P34 2022 | DDC 621.4/5309764—dc23/eng/20220215
LC record available at https://lccn.loc.gov/2022002402

Printed in Canada
FRI
23 24 25 26 27 28 29 30 / 9 8 7 6 5 4 3 2

Texas Tech University Press
Box 41037
Lubbock, Texas 79409-1037 USA
800.832.4042
ttup@ttu.edu
www.ttupress.org

Dedicated to Charla and Brint
and especially to
Blake, Burke, Aasra, and River

Beside
That
Windmill

The sun greeted a new day.

Its warmth spread across miles of golden, waving grass —

just as it had done for hundreds of years.

That beautiful, tall grass swayed in the wind,

like rolling ocean waves.

Nothing else seemed to be there.

The Great Plains, right in the middle of the United States,

was mostly flat, mostly dry, mostly empty.

However, a closer look revealed some Native Americans
living by small streams.
They knew how hard it was to find water
on the Great Plains.
But beneath that ground lay a huge aquifer
containing vast amounts of water,
waiting to be tapped.

Then something happened.

In 1854, a clever engineer named Daniel Halladay designed the American windmill.

This windmill took its name from its source of power – the wind.

And this windmill brought water from deep in the ground to the thirsty Plains.

This invention of the American windmill made it possible

for the railroad to stretch all across the United States.

Railroads needed water to power their steam engines.

The engines could only go short distances before refilling with water.

Once the ingenious windmill had been invented,

it was the most valuable possession for farmers and ranchers.

Families could now live in this mostly dry, treeless place.

With a windmill pumping water to the top of the ground,

the people could have water

for their animals, gardens, and themselves.

Over the years, more and more windmills dotted the Plains,
as people settled there.
Farmers moved their families, dug water wells,
built windmills over the wells, and grew crops.
Ranchers also dug water wells and put windmills
in place to water their cattle.

Years later my story about living beside a windmill began . . .

On the first day of summer, my parents, my brother, Carl, and I loaded up our 1953 Oldsmobile.

We drove 135 miles northwest from Seymour, Texas,

to a desolate, flat, windy farming area between the small towns of Matador and Floydada.

Just for the summer my family lived in an old, white farmhouse

that had no water, no bathroom, and no electricity.

Nothing else around that place could be seen — no neighbors or trees or anything.

Only the house and beside it was that windmill,

standing very tall with its fan wheel spinning in the wind.

It was a lot of work to live in a house with no water.

So guess who had to fetch water for the house?

Carrying heavy buckets filled with water from that windmill was not an easy job.

My mom would say,

"Don, it's your turn to bring me some water so that I can cook dinner."

Or wash dishes or clean those dusty old rooms in that house.

I would think, "Oh, Mom, not again."

The windmill pumped water as long as the wind blew gently.

That wonderful water would come up the long pipe in the ground,

flow into a barrel,

and then pour into a large round tank for the animals.

The cattle, rabbits, birds, insects, and frogs

all depended on the water from that windmill,

just like we did.

At the windmill there was a metal dipper with a long handle.

And any time I was thirsty

I could grab that dipper and

catch the cold water tumbling out of the pipe.

That was the coolest drink of water I could ever want.

The cold water was caught in an old barrel and used for other things, too,

like cooling a watermelon.

Luckily, I could climb to the platform of that windmill any time I wanted.

From the top, I felt as if I could see forever,

even some tall grain elevators 20 miles away in Floydada.

Sitting up there I felt like a bird drifting in the breeze.

"Wow," I would think. "I'm almost as high as those hawks circling around."

The things I really liked to see were the cattle trails

leading from the pastures to the windmill.

The trails would start far away and wind around bushes

and all end at the windmill – the paths looking like spokes on a wheel.

Not everything about having a windmill was fun.
Sometimes the windmill broke and no water would come out.
My dad would say, "Boys, we have to work on the windmill today."
We had to pull part of the pump out from the bottom of the well
and replace the worn-out leathers.[*]
Repairing the windmill took hours of work in the hot sun
before we could get a drink of cool, fresh water. "Whew!"

[*] See pump diagram.

Late every evening Carl and I bathed

in that COLD water in the cattle tank.

We never wanted to plunge into that tank full of cold windmill water.

But something made us do it.

We would hurriedly strip off our clothes.

Carl would yell, "Don, jump in before the mosquitoes get you!"

SPLASH!

We would quickly JUMP into that very cold water

to keep from getting so many mosquito bites.

The best part of having a windmill close
was how it sounded at night.
The window next to my bed was open and
I could look out and see the windmill in the moonlight.
The wind usually blew gently then,
and kept the windmill turning all night long.
As the windmill pumped water to the top of the ground,
it made a slow rhythmic CLANK, CLANK, CLANK sound.
And that sound in the night wind
would sing me to sleep.

Pump diagram

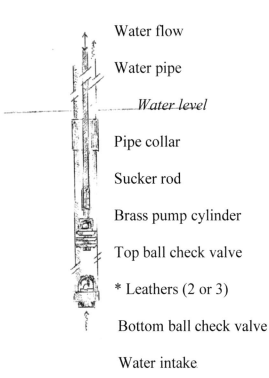

Water flow

Water pipe

Water level

Pipe collar

Sucker rod

Brass pump cylinder

Top ball check valve

* Leathers (2 or 3)

Bottom ball check valve

Water intake

As the wind blows and turns the fan blades, the gearbox causes the sucker rod (reaching down to the pump and water table) to move up and down. It also moves the leathers.

Windmill down stroke: Bottom pump check valve closes and top pump check valve opens, allowing the brass cylinder to be filled with water above the top check valve.

Windmill up stroke: Top pump check valve closes, forcing water to flow up the water pipe to the surface. Also, the bottom check pump valve opens, allowing water to be sucked into cylinder.

These two stroke cycles repeat.

Afterword

Windmills lost much of their importance for many farmers and ranchers after 1936. The availability of rural electricity and the invention of electric motors to pump water to the top of the ground gradually became common. These motors were easier than a windmill to keep running. Like other inventions, many of the windmills were eventually replaced by something newer and better. Remote areas of the Great Plains, however, still rely on windmills to furnish water for livestock, crops, and people. Traveling north and south through the middle of the United States, you will find windmill wheels turning quickly in the wind, reminding us of the important role they played in settling the Great Plains.

About the Authors

Minda and Don Parks collaborated for this historical and personal story about windmills. Beside That Windmill is Don's true story about spending summers on a farm that had no modern conveniences.

 Minda Parks, an enthusiastic reader of adult and children's books, encourages others to read. Mrs. Parks, now retired, taught in Texas public schools in Wichita Falls and Midland. Her teaching career was spent in the classroom and as a reading specialist. She has degrees from Texas Tech University and the University of Texas Permian Basin. She and Don live in Midland, Texas, and have two adult children and four grandchildren.

 Don Parks is a professional artist and a veteran who also had careers as an agricultural economist and a trust banker. Parks, largely self-taught, studied art and painted in the evenings after working in his other professions. His subject matter portrays his time spent outdoors as a boy on a farm and as an adult studying nature, such as clouds and sunsets. Parks has degrees from Texas Tech University. His website is www.donparksfineart.com.

Author photos courtesy of John Watson.